SOUNDS EASY!

a phonics workbook

for beginning E.S.L.

students

by sharron bassano

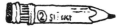

illustrated by craig cornell

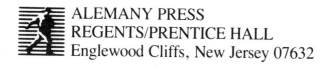

ALEMANY PRESS
REGENTS/PRENTICE HALL
Englewood Cliffs, New Jersey 07632

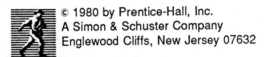 © 1980 by Prentice-Hall, Inc.
A Simon & Schuster Company
Englewood Cliffs, New Jersey 07632

Printed in the United States of America

10 9 8 7 6 5

ISBN 0-13-829821-1

Prentice-Hall International (UK) Limited, *London*
Prentice-Hall of Australia Pty. Limited, *Sydney*
Prentice-Hall Canada Inc., *Toronto*
Prentice-Hall Hispanoamericana, S.A., *Mexico*
Prentice-Hall of India Private Limited, *New Delhi*
Prentice-Hall of Japan, Inc., *Tokyo*
Simon & Schuster Asia Pte. Ltd., *Signapore*
Editora Prentice-Hall do Brasil, Ltda., *Rio de Janeiro*

Who's this book for?

This workbook was created especially for beginning ESL students of non-academic backgrounds - students who are often mystified by texts, exercise books and work sheets. Our aim is to simply introduce eleven English vowel sounds to non-native speakers and give them practice at recognition of the letters and combinations of letters that most often produce these sounds. The exercises we present will help to teach oral and written discrimination and offer opportunities to listen, read, write, and pronounce. It is not our intention to present an all-inclusive, comprehensive English phonics program. You will not find arrows, charts or diagrams. There are no detailed instructions for the students or complicated spelling rules or fine print.

We hope that our plain, uncluttered format will eliminate the confusion or anxiety often experienced by semi-literate students when faced with ordinary workbooks. We have included only the "basics" for two reasons: Only you, the teacher, can know how much 'explanation' your students can handle or how much they require. Only you know the best way to ensure comprehension in your students, based upon your knowledge of their goals. We hope our format will allow some basic spelling rules to be inferred or deduced by your students, however, we leave instruction technique mostly up to you. We invite you to expand or adapt these pages to your particular style of teaching and for your particular student population.

Sounds Easy is intended to bring feelings of immediate success and achievement through its easy-to-follow, pleasing to look at pages, and to encourage continued study well beyond this introductory book.

How to use this book.

PICTURE PAGE

Each of the eleven vowel sounds is introduced with a **picture page** to allow your students to offer something they already know to the class. Let your students "brainstorm" the labels to each picture, asking "Who knows the name of one of the pictures?" or "Who knows number six?". As the students volunteer what they know or guess, write the words on the board and ask them to copy them under the pictures. (Rarely will you have to tell your students any of the pictures – especially in a multicultural class or a multilevel class – and we know that all classes are multilevel!)

After the pictures have all been labeled, read them through all together or have a couple of volunteers read them. Then you might try a sort of "bingo", calling out the labels at random having the students "X" them out. Those that read quickly will look for the words, others will go by the picture, and still others will look at their neighbor's paper to see what he or she is doing – and that's all okay – we simply want to reinforce.

READ

After your students have had the opportunity to relate a specific and isolated vowel sound to a visual image, they are then given a chance to read a list of words containing that sound as rein- forcement, as practice and as confidence builder. Tell them that, for the moment, meaning is not important – the focus is on the guessing game of sounding out the words based on what they have seen on the previous page. Have the students read along with you in chorus or in small groups. Possibly someone may want to volunteer to read alone, or you might want to pair off students, having one read to the other in a random order while his or her partner points to them. Most of the words in the **read** section are common every-day words that would most surely come up in books one or two of your text series; others are more obscure, but are given as practice and to further illustrate any rule consistency.

WRITE

As the third step, you will dictate twelve of the words on the list at random for your students to respond to according to their level. They will search for the word you pronounce and either underline it or copy it in the spaces provided. Those who are more advanced may want to cover the list and write what they hear from memory or by sounding out the word. When your dictation is finished, write the words in order on the board (or have a student do it) and go over them once more.

TROUBLEMAKERS

Troublemakers are words that don't "follow the rule" - words that the students must memorize. Practice these words a few times, and, if possible, have the students write near equivalents in their native alphabet or sound system. (i.e. says = ses, hi = jai, for Spanish speakers.)

COMPARE

The **compare** sections are made up mostly of minimal pair words, placed randomly, from which your students will have to choose for the dictation. This gives them the opportunity to use their discriminatory skills gained in the preliminary exercises, and to draw on any sort of rule for spelling or pronunciation that they have become aware of. The initial **compare** sections include the long and short pronunciation of one letter - i.e. ă / ā or ŏ / ŏ. Pages 32 through 41 make comparisons between commonly confused minimal pairs such as ă / ŏ and ī / ĕ, and offer extra visual references.

REVIEW

Five pages of review are included to offer a greater challenge and to evaluate learnings. These sections are made up of minimal pairs, but contain a mixture of all eleven vowels sounds to choose from in the dictation and reading. Upon completion of this section, it will be apparent who still needs more assistance in recognition and discrimination of sounds and spelling patterns.

SENTENCE PRACTICE

Several sections have been included that offer short controlled sentences for reading practice. These sentences focus on the vowel sound(s) being practiced in that particular lesson, and should be easy to 'de-code'! If your students are not yet at a level to derive meaning from the sentences, you may be able to make meanings clear through actions or object manipulation or pictures. If not, we see no harm in brief 'no-sense' practice of English pronunciation and rhythm for its own sake. (If your own particular philosophy finds no use in this lesson section, by all means, skip over it!) For students with good functional comprehension but few reading/writing skills, these short sentences will be a fine extra reinforcement of their learnings.

THE BOX

Above each **read** section you will find a small box. This box is a special place where the students might make a notation of the vowel sound being featured, writing it in a near equivalent in their own alphabet or sound system. (i.e. - i = ai , a = ei for Spanish speakers.) This is to assist them in their home practice and avoid confusion when there is no one around to remind or model for them.

We hope you and your students enjoy our spelling and/or phonics workbook and experience beginning reading and writing English in a low-stress, light-hearted manner. The above ideas are only a few ways in which you might use this book and we invite you to experiment and expand the activities using your imagination and creativity. Please let us know of your successes!

Sharron Bassano
Craig Cornell

d

Contents

e

1.

A

6. pan

9. sack

16. bag

tag

A

Read

am	fat	pan
at	gas	ran
as	had	sad
bad	jam	sack
can	mad	happy
cap	map	tack
dad	pad	van

Write

1. _____
2. _____
3. _____
4. _____
5. _____
6. _____

7. _____
8. _____
9. _____
10. _____
11. _____
12. _____

Trouble Makers

what
was
many
any

A

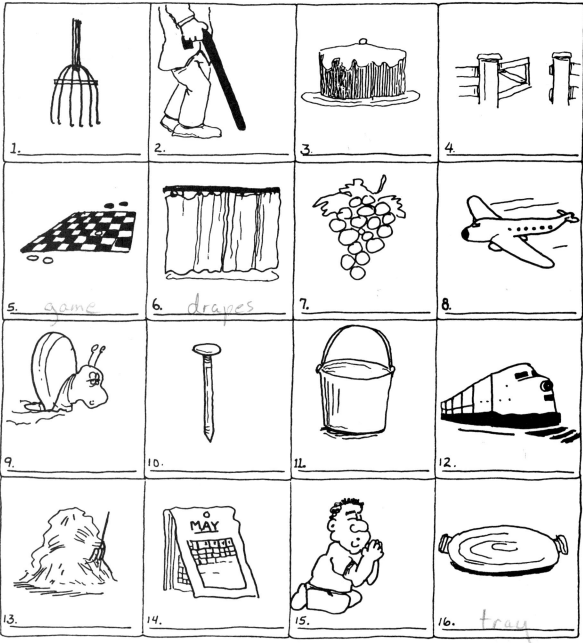

1. _____

2. _____

3. _____

4. _____

5. game

6. drapes

7. _____

8. _____

9. _____

10. _____

11. _____

12. _____

13. _____

14. _____

15. _____

16. tray

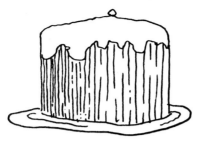

A·E   AI   AY

Read

ate	aid	day
bake	bait	hay
cape	chain	jay
face	maid	pay
game	mail	play
gave	pain	say
lane	rain	stay
make	train	tray

Write

1. _____
2. _____
3. _____
4. _____
5. _____
6. _____
7. _____
8. _____
9. _____
10. _____
11. _____
12. _____

Trouble Makers

have   said
are   says
              again

A   A·E / AI / AY

Compare

man	sad	main	tape
pad	fat	pay *pail*	paid
lack	mad	made	rain
ran	tap	lake	fail
hat	pal	say	hay
		fate	*hate*

Write

1. _____   7. _____

2. _____   8. _____

3. _____   9. _____

4. _____   10. _____

5. _____   11. _____

6. _____   12. _____

Read

Make a hat.
A man paid.
The rain came today.
A cat ran.
Play the tape.
Sam is fat.

1.

2.

3.

4.

5.

6. pick

7.

8.

9. MILK

10.

11.

12.

13.

14.

15. pig

16. 6

Read

is	his	sit
it	kick	sip
in	mitt	six
big	kitchen	thin
bit	pick	this
did	pig	window
fin	pin	will
him	rim	zip

Write

1. _____
2. _____
3. _____
4. _____
5. _____
6. _____

7. _____
8. _____
9. _____
10. _____
11. _____
12. _____

Trouble Makers

hi
find

9 I

1.

2.

3.

4.

5.

6.

7.

8.

9.

10.

11.

12.

13.

14.

15.

16.

9

I·E   **IE / IGH**

Read

I	mile	pie
bike	mine	tie
dime	nine	lie
drive	ride	
fine	size	fight
five	smile	sight
like	time	tight
line	white	might

Write

1. _____
2. _____
3. _____
4. _____
5. _____
6. _____
7. _____
8. _____
9. _____
10. _____
11. _____
12. _____

Trouble Makers

piece   friend
believe
field

9

I   I·E / IE / IGH

Compare

bid	sit	like	hide
bit	sin	sight	light
lit	win	tile	bite
hid	till	bide	sign
kit	lick	kite	wine

Write

1. _____   7. _____

2. _____   8. _____

3. _____   9. _____

4. _____   10. _____

5. _____   11. _____

6. _____   12. _____

Read

Sit in the window.
Sip the wine.
I like it.
Is this the kitchen?
Hide his bike.
I lit the light.

E

1.

2.

3.

4.

5.

6.

7.

8.

9.

10.

11.

12.

13.

14.

15.

16.

E

Read

Ed	men	yellow
bed	net	yes
egg	pep	yet
fell	red	elephant
get	sell	bell
jet	ten	them
leg	web	best
letter	well	hello

Write

1. _____   7. _____

2. _____   8. _____

3. _____   9. _____

4. _____   10. _____

5. _____   11. _____

6. _____   12. _____

Trouble Makers

they	we
the	he
	she
	me

E

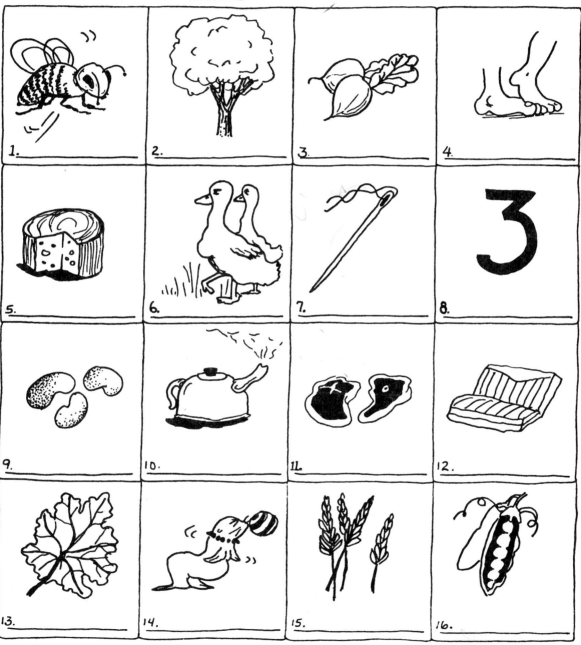

1.

2.

3.

4.

5.

6.

7.

8.

9.

10.

11.

12.

13.

14.

15.

16.

EE   EA

Read

free	feel	flea	please
see	green	pea	cream
three	keep	sea	mean
tree	meet	tea	peach
beef	need	eat	read
cheek	sheep	beach	speak
cheese	sleep	cheap	teacher
feed	teeth	clean	weak

Write

1. _____
2. _____
3. _____
4. _____
5. _____
6. _____

7. _____
8. _____
9. _____
10. _____
11. _____
12. _____

Trouble Makers

head	been	great	ocean
bread		steak	beautiful
thread		break	
instead			
dead			

15

E   EE / EA

Compare

bed	fell	weed	bead
bet	men	beat	feed
den	peck	feel	reed
fed	sell	dean	mean
red	wed	peek	seal

Write

1. _____   7. _____
2. _____   8. _____
3. _____   9. _____
4. _____   10. _____
5. _____   11. _____
6. _____   12. _____

Read

I see seven men.
He sells beads.
She sleeps in the best bed.
Three sheep eat weeds.
Do elephants eat peas and eggs?

1.

2.

3.

4.

5.

6.

7.

8.

9.

10.

11.

12.

13.

14.

15.

16.

0

Read

Bob	mop	dot
box	not	fog
cot	on	hog
doll	off	jog
got	rod	lock
hot	top	block
job	tot	nod
lot	cob	rob

Write

1. _____   7. _____

2. _____   8. _____

3. _____   9. _____

4. _____   10. _____

5. _____   11. _____

6. _____   12. _____

Trouble Makers

go	do	most	color
so	who	both	doctor
off	you	only	young
			cousin
			country

O

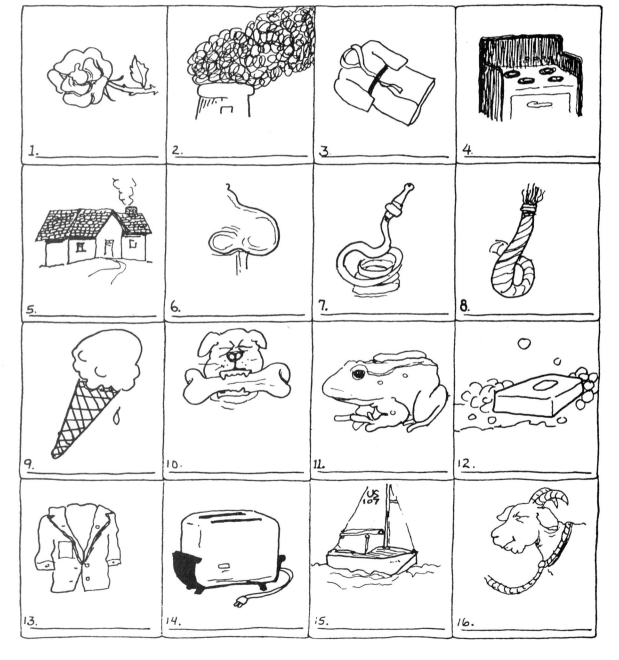

1.

2.

3.

4.

5.

6.

7.

8.

9.

10.

11.

12.

13.

14.

15.

16.

OE OW   O·E   OA ☐

Read

toe	broke	cloak
Joe	close	coal
hoe	dome	foam
woe	drove	groan
mow	hole	load
low	joke	road
throw	lone	soap
blow	nose	toast

Write

1. _____   7. _____

2. _____   8. _____

3. _____   9. _____

4. _____   10. _____

5. _____   11. _____

6. _____   12. _____

Trouble Makers

love	some	prove	gone
done		move	women
come		lose	
none		shoe	
one			
does			

O   O·E / OA

Compare

cŏp	sŏp	sōak	code
cod	mop	robe	road
cot	not	dole	mope
doll	rob rod	coat	note
rob	sock	cope	soap

Write

1. _____   7. _____

2. _____   8. _____

3. _____   9. _____

4. _____   10. _____

5. _____   11. _____

6. _____   12. _____

Read

Jon broke the clock.
The socks are in the box.
Bob got a coat.
Don't throw the soap.
Tom drove on an old road.

U

1.

2.

3.

4.

5.

6.

7.

8.

9.

10.

11.

12.

13.

14.

15.

16.

U ☐

Read

us	jut	under
up	mutt	umbrella
bud	nun	understand
bun	pup	truck
cut	rub	sun
duck	sum	dug
gum	run	study
hug	dull	bucket

Write

1. _____
2. _____
3. _____
4. _____
5. _____
6. _____

7. _____
8. _____
9. _____
10. _____
11. _____
12. _____

Trouble Makers

bull	usual	put	busy
full	human		business
pull			

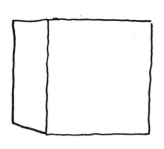

U

1.

2.

3.

4.

5.

6.

7.

8.

9.

10.

11.

12.

13.

14.

15.

16.

UE   **U·E**   **UI**   **U·E**

Read

true	dude	fruit	cube
blue	dune	suit	cute
due	flume	juice	fume
flue	prune		fuse
	plume		huge
	rule		mule
	tube		mute
	tune		use

Write

1. _____   7. _____

2. _____   8. _____

3. _____   9. _____

4. _____   10. _____

5. _____   11. _____

6. _____   12. _____

Trouble Makers

buy   building

25

U

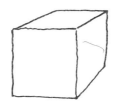

UI / U·E

Compare

us	cub	ruin	rube
cut	duck	tube	use
mull	jut	mule	cube
but	run	duke	butte
tub	rub	cute	jute

Write

1. _____ 7. _____

2. _____ 8. _____

3. _____ 9. _____

4. _____ 10. _____

5. _____ 11. _____

6. _____ 12. _____

Read

Cut the cube of butter.
Use the umbrella.
Hug the duck.
The students understand.
The fruit juice is for Sue.

A

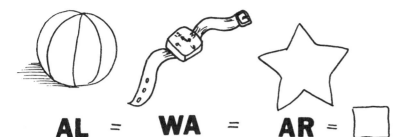

AL = **WA** = **AR** = ▢

Read

all	wall	bar
fall	water	far
call	want	cart
ball	watch	market
tall	wash	park
~~talk~~	wad	star
~~walk~~	watt	hard
	walk	

Write

1. _____   7. _____

2. _____   8. _____

3. _____   9. _____

4. _____   10. _____

5. _____   11. _____

6. _____   12. _____

Trouble Makers

shall   *talk*
pal
calendar
valley
gallon

A

AL / WA / AR

Compare

as	fad	fall	tar
tap	ran	water	start
can	happy	car	wash
map	tab	watch	tall
sat	has	salt	wall

Write

1. _____   7. _____

2. _____   8. _____

3. _____   9. _____

4. _____   10. _____

5. _____   11. _____

6. _____   12. _____

Read

Jan is always happy.
It's all salt water.
Carl sat on the map!
Start the car.
Watch the tall man.

REVIEW A

29

Compare

am	all	ate	ail
water	gas	game	Gail
bad	hall	father	shall
have	gave	want	pad
paid	hail	bade	ant

Write

1. _____
2. _____
3. _____
4. _____
5. _____
6. _____
7. _____
8. _____
9. _____
10. _____
11. _____
12. _____

Read

Ann has a table.
Father pays for the gas.
Hail a taxi.
The water is bad.
Has Jane come back?
Can the baby play?

9

I

A

Compare

bike	gripe	grape	glade
file	lime	lake	main
glide	mine	fail	race
like	rice	tame	bait
time	bite	bake	lame

Write

1. _____   7. _____

2. _____   8. _____

3. _____   9. _____

4. _____   10. _____

5. _____   11. _____

6. _____   12. _____

Read

I like grapes.
David likes lime-ade.
The bike is mine.
Bake a cake.
Nina takes pie.

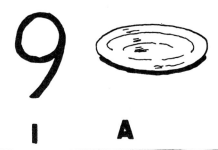

31

9

I   A

Compare

add	hid	kick	aid
case	past	tape	hide
did	mice	dad	mace
bit;	dime	bite	bait
wife	save	dame	had

Write

1. _____
2. _____
3. _____
4. _____
5. _____
6. _____
7. _____
8. _____
9. _____
10. _____
11. _____
12. _____

Read

Kick the tire.
Hide the dime.
Jack kisses his wife.
Tape the paper.
Time has passed.
Dad drank the wine.

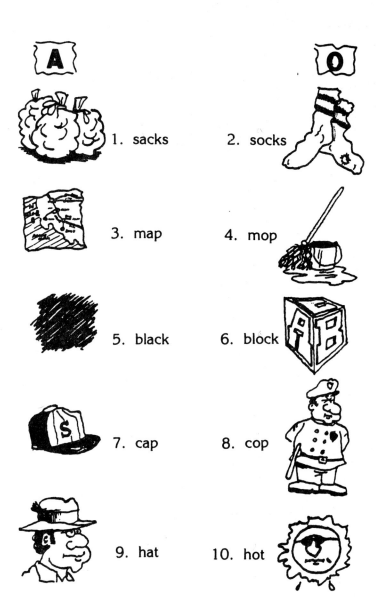

A   O

1. sacks   2. socks

3. map   4. mop

5. black   6. block

7. cap   8. cop

9. hat   10. hot

A   **O**

Compare

an	hag	ox	bog
ax	tap	hog	cop
bag	tag	tog	pod
sack	pad	sock	top
cap	cab	on	cob

Write

1. _____
2. _____
3. _____
4. _____
5. _____
6. _____

7. _____
8. _____
9. _____
10. _____
11. _____
12. _____

Read

That hog is fat.
Don's cap is black.
The sock is in the bag.
The tag is on the box.
The cat ran to Tom.

I

E

1. ship

2. sheep

3. chick

4. cheek

5. hill

6. heel

7. fist

8. feast

9. slip

10. sleep

11. bit

12. beet

I   **E**

Compare

bid	pill	lead	feet
bin	ship	deep	bead
did	sit	bean	seat
dip	hip	deed	sheep
fit	lid	heap	peal

Write

1. _____
2. _____
3. _____
4. _____
5. _____
6. _____

7. _____
8. _____
9. _____
10. _____
11. _____
12. _____

Read

Six sheep eat weeds.
Did it fit?
Eat these beans, please!
Sit on this seat.
His feet are in the sink!

| A | E |

 1. pan   2. pen

 3. ladder   4. letter

 5. man   6. men

 7. ham   8. hem

 9. bat   10. bet

A

E

37

Compare

bad	man	peck	hem
bag	pat	gem	led
ham	tan	beg	pet
jam	sat	set	bed
lad	pack	men	ten

Write

1. _____
2. _____
3. _____
4. _____
5. _____
6. _____

7. _____
8. _____
9. _____
10. _____
11. _____
12. _____

Read

Helen has her hat.
Get the jam.
Pet the hens.
Ten happy men sat in the taxi!
Pat went to bed.

A

 U

1. cap

2. cup

3. bag

4. bug

5. hat

6. hut

7. cat

8. cut

9. cab

10. cub

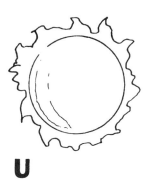

U

A

Compare

bud	luck	hag	tag
cub	mud	as	cab
fun	rug	lack	bad
gull	tub	mad	fan
hug	us	rag	gal

Write

1. _____   7. _____
2. _____   8. _____
3. _____   9. _____
4. _____   10. _____
5. _____   11. _____
6. _____   12. _____

Read

Hug that cat.
Run to the taxi fast!
Dan is a lucky man.
What is that under the rug?

U   **O**

 1. hug   2. hog

 3. cup   4. cop

 5. run   6. Ron

 7. cut   8. cot

 9. hut   10. hot

U

O

Compare

bug	jug	cod	lock
bucks	mum	boss	box
bus	nut	bog	jog
luck	sub	sob	not
hut	cud	hot	mom

Write

1. _____
2. _____
3. _____
4. _____
5. _____
6. _____

7. _____
8. _____
9. _____
10. _____
11. _____
12. _____

Read

Lock the box.
Bud's boss is upstairs.
Jog around the block.
My umbrella is on the bus!

42

Review

Compare

post	bad	wave	chose
shape	mop	hit	pod
lick	bite	pass	wise
paste	bid	chase	wife
ship	mope	hate	pad

Write

1. _____ 7. _____

2. _____ 8. _____

3. _____ 9. _____

4. _____ 10. _____

5. _____ 11. _____

6. _____ 12. _____

Read

Lick the stamp.
Mail the letter.
Mop the kitchen.
Bite the apple.
Fix the bike.

Review

Compare

odd	tape	kit	led
rag	pose	nine	fell
ox	dive	be	pat
add	kite	lad	dove
lid	rig	fail	Kate

Write

1. _____
2. _____
3. _____
4. _____
5. _____
6. _____

7. _____
8. _____
9. _____
10. _____
11. _____
12. _____

Read

Be happy!
Kate fell on the step.
Add the milk.
Stop the tape.
He feels lazy.

44

Review

Compare

zone	wag	chin	we
music	duck	gaze	nest
Tom	shine	Dick	wig
back	game	mile	mail
woke	sheep	wake	ship

Write

1. _____   7. _____

2. _____   8. _____

3. _____   9. _____

4. _____   10. _____

5. _____   11. _____

6. _____   12. _____

Read

Listen to the music.
He woke the baby.
Shine the windows.
Walk a mile.
Send the package.

Review

Compare

race	cat	hide	sit
hope	top	me	let
cute	luck	rice	hid
sight	lit	cut	lack
lick	let	rose	hop

Write

1. _____   7. _____

2. _____   8. _____

3. _____   9. _____

4. _____   10. _____

5. _____   11. _____

6. _____   12. _____

Read

The sailboats are racing.
What a cute cat!
Cut the meat for the soup.
A rose is in the vase.
Eat the rice.
He plays hide and seek.

46

Review

Compare

sell	him	job	take
win	pipe	buzz	home
scene	bath	seal	hem
tick	wine	pit	boss
bass	pup	jam	Jim

Write

1. _____
2. _____
3. _____
4. _____
5. _____
6. _____

7. _____
8. _____
9. _____
10. _____
11. _____
12. _____

Read

She sells flowers.
Catch that fish!
Let's go home.
Jim likes Susan.
Bees buzz.

Answer Key

Page 1	Page 3	Page 6	Page 8	Page 11
Lamp	Rake	Ink	Sign	Net
Bat	Cane	Lip	Fight	Pen
Man	Cake	Sink	Night	Hen
Cap	Gate	Ring	Light	Egg
Ax	Game	Lid	Fire	Ten
Pan	Drapes	Pick	Five	Nest
Fan	Grapes	Dish	Tire	Bell
Hat	Plane	Gift	Bike	Men
Sack	Snail	Milk	Pipe	Belt
Back	Nail	Ship	Stripe	Vest
Can	Pail	Fish	Nine	Tent
Ham	Train	Chin	Dime	Leg
Flag	Hay	Pin	Line	Bed
Tag	May	Hill	Pie	Desk
Cat	Pray	Pig	Tie	Web
Bag	Tray	Six	Time	Pencil

Page 13	Page 16	Page 18	Page 21	Page 23	Page 26
Bee	Top	Rose	Sun	Cube	Call
Tree	Spot	Smoke	Duck	Tube	Car
Beet	Clock	Robe	Jump	Fuse	Watch
Feet	Dog	Stove	Bus	Ruler	Ball
Cheese	Blocks	Home	Nut	Plume	Walk
Geese	Fox	Nose	Cup	June	Talk
Needle	Log	Hose	Jug	Student	Wall
Three	Rocket	Rope	Drum	Music	Water
Bean	Ox	Cone	Button	Mule	Tall
Tea	Lock	Bone	Tub	Fumes	Wash
Meat	Socks	Toad	Truck	Juice	Bar
Seat	Bottle	Soap	Bug	Fruit	Star
Leaf	Box	Coat	Gun	Suit	Cart
Seal	Rock	Toaster	Brush	Perfume	Card
Wheat	Pot	Boat	Trunk	Flute	Park
Peas	Cot	Goat	Rug	Glue	Market

HASLETT COMMUNITY EDUCATION
ESL Program / UMHE
1118 South Harrison Road
East Lansing, Michigan 48823 USA
Telephone (517) 337-8353